MW00979927

75 Traits of Great Leaders

75 Traits of Great Leaders

How to Recognize if You've Got What It Takes to Lead

A one-wisdom-per-page inspirational book

T. C. Waisman, M.A.

75 Traits of Great Leaders
Copyright © 2015 by (Know Thyself Publishing)

All rights reserved. No part of this book may be reproduced or transmitted in any
form or by any means without written permission from the author.

TITLE ID:
5134116

ISBN-13: 9781505245929

ISBN-10: 1505245923
Library of Congress Control Number: 2015913291
CreateSpace Independent Publishing Platform
North Charleston, South Carolina
Printed in Canada by Know Thyself Publishing

Dedication

Three extraordinary people helped make this book a reality. My daughter, Dylan-Sunshine, you are my heart, my teacher, fierce advocate, one-woman comedy troupe, and the reason I aspire to be better in the world. Thank you for believing that your mama can do anything.

Dean, you are my partner, father of our daughter, my greatest supporter, and my hero. Thank you for having faith in us over the 25 entertaining years of our marriage.

My best friend, editor, wise woman and godmother to my daughter: Sunshine Kesey. You encourage me to believe in myself every single day. I thank you deeply for your friendship.

Endless gratitude to my extraordinary family for the love and support through the years. Our gregarious family dinners are the stuff of legends.

Profound thanks to Julie Hamilton, Terry Ramsey, and Alison van Buuren. Through the journey of our careers you shared your wisdom freely and you encouraged me to write this book. You are extraordinary women and wonderful friends.

Finally, to my Saltspring Island cabin gals: thanks for the insightful conversations, deep friendships, and endless laughter.

Preface

After decades of coaching and training executive clients in the art of being adaptive leaders, my inspirational clients asked me to write down some of the gems that I've learned along the way. This book was written from the learning my leaders and I uncovered together in our coaching relationships and from the wisdom of the great leaders whom I studied in my master's degree program on leadership.

This book's format honors the fast-paced world we live in by offering wisdom in short bursts. Each chapter offers just one trait on each page. Feel free to open the book and read any chapter that fits your needs at that moment.

75 Traits of Great Leaders is meant to encourage you to try on new leadership thoughts and skills in order to see how they can improve your leadership. I ask you to read with an open mind. Be adventurous, stretch yourself, and try to broaden aspects of your leadership. Leave behind what doesn't work for you, and keep moving toward your personal leadership goals.

Introduction

> I've learned that people will forget what you said, people will forget what you did, but people will never forget how you made them feel.
>
> —MAYA ANGELOU

75 Traits of Great Leaders is a collection of the most important qualities that many great leaders possess. Collected throughout years of research, these seventy-five traits are meant as a guide for you to use as you develop your own leadership capacity and the leadership capacity of those around you.

The concept for this book was developed when I returned to my small village in Fiji to write my master's thesis on the traits of leaders in our ancient culture and how these could be transferred to organizations today. I learned quickly that our villages consider leaders to be those who rise to the occasion as the need arises. Leadership is not a static role in villages; it is adaptive to the environment, and each person is capable of leading if they possess the leadership trait the group needs most in that moment. I began to investigate this further, and I made the realization that all of us have the potential for great leadership if we know what traits we can access within ourselves when the need arises.

Through further research I learned that there are seventy-five characteristics of exceptional leaders that cross cultural, racial, economic, and historical barriers. All of these traits are based on the foundation of respect and compassion. No one leader possesses all of these qualities, but every strong leader possesses some. Use this book as a reference point for your personal growth by marking the traits that you already have and noticing the ones that you'd like to add to your leadership competency. You can use the action plan on the last page to help you develop the traits that will benefit you the most in your particular leadership practice. You can also use the action plan in the self-assessment portion of your yearly organizational performance review to show evidence of how you will grow yourself as a leader.

One

Inspire Others

**Our chief want is someone who will inspire us
to be what we know we could be.**

—RALPH WALDO EMERSON

L eadership is often mistaken as a natural extension of a title or a role. That just isn't the case. Certainly, a title can mean you're in charge of a team, but it doesn't automatically mean you have become a leader.

A leader is someone who can motivate others to follow them toward an outcome. The operative word in that sentence is "motivate." Great leaders, such as Nelson Mandela, Malala Yousafzai, or Mother Teresa, motivate others through inspiration. They help people transform their lives by inspiring them to make lifelong changes.

It's true that some have found success through threatening or cajoling people to make a change; but there isn't any motivation to make those changes stick, so they often end up being short-term changes with negative consequences.

Inspiring others is important to a strong leader; it shows that people believe in you enough to be influenced by you and trust you enough to lead them. Use your leadership wisely; aspire to inspire others.

Two

Stay Curious

**The important thing is not to stop questioning.
Curiosity has its own reason for existing.**

—ALBERT EINSTEIN

What is the natural antidote to being judgmental? You guessed it: staying curious.

Like with your body, you need to work at keeping this attribute moving and flexible. If you don't, you'll find yourself atrophying into a version of the grumpy old character Carl in the kids' movie *Up*.

Staying curious allows you to be open to the world and keeps you present in the moment rather than living in the past or jumping ahead to the future.

Here's how you know you're atrophying: In conversations, do you catch yourself stating everything as if it's a fact? Are you annoyed that others don't know as much as you do? Do you have strong opinions about absolutely everything? If so, you could be losing your sense of curiosity.

Lucky for you, we were all born curious; that's what inspired us to crawl, walk, and, eventually, run. We were curious about our world and had no inhibitions about reaching for everything.

It's in you. As a leader, allow yourself to begin practicing curiosity again. Let go of knowing; ask questions. Notice your world with new curious eyes. Say the words "I'm not sure. What do you think?" Follow other people's perspective in conversations, and ask curious questions to try to understand them more. Let go of the need to show how much you know. Be a fan of others, not just a person looking for fans. As the R&B group En Vogue once sang, "Free your mind...the rest will follow."

Three

Work on Emotional Intelligence

I think, for leadership positions, emotional intelligence is more important than cognitive intelligence.

—John Mackey

EQ, or emotional quotient, may seem to be a buzzword in leadership these days, but there's a very compelling reason for it. As confident as we are now that global warming exists, leadership experts now understand that IQ doesn't matter as much in leadership as EQ does.

In the past, it was enough to have gone through the education system to secure a leadership position, but it was never guaranteed that a person with the right degree could actually lead people. In fact, we've learned that while a high IQ serves well in the education system, leaders lacking high EQ are ineffective at best and dangerous at worst.

Leaders with low EQ have little understanding of how relationships work and, as a result, tend to lose good people from their teams. Relationships are the basis of leadership, and your level of success depends on how you relate to others. Thankfully, bullying, passive aggressiveness, and aggressiveness are no longer tolerated from those in leadership positions.

Organizations look for someone with an education *and* a strong EQ. They look for traits such as compassion, open-mindedness, an understanding of self, an understanding of the separation of self and other, and an ability to see your personal limitations. In short, organizations are looking for your emotional awareness of yourself and others in the world.

Luckily it's never too late to work on these traits. Start where you are. Get a professional EQ assessment done, and develop a plan for your learning.

Four

Have Integrity

Integrity is doing the right thing even when no one is watching.

—C. S. LEWIS

What does it mean to have integrity?

Having integrity as a leader means having morals and ethics that act as an internal compass to guide you to make good decisions for yourself and your team. It means putting people and relationships first and foremost in your decision-making process, and it means understanding that doing the right thing for yourself and your stakeholders is the sure way of building long-term trust, thus ensuring that you and your stakeholders are getting the best results you can together.

Integrity doesn't mean promoting your own personal agenda over that of others. If you find that you're having a personal crisis between your values and that of your company, then it's time to seek wisdom from others—those who hold your perspective and those who don't—and be prepared to leave your position if you feel called to do so.

Having integrity within an organization is your leadership challenge. Consider deeply the needs of your stakeholders, your company, and the individuals in your team. Continue to develop your integrity by questioning your motives, surrounding yourself with a team holding differing perspectives, and being open to learning other points of view.

Five

Understand Your Impact

If you think you're too small to make an impact, try going to bed with a mosquito [in the room].

—Anita Roddick

In a perfect world, people around us would take our words and actions in exactly the way we mean them. Often, however, our words and actions are received in a shockingly different way than we intend.

Being a strong leader means working hard to be clear about your intentions and then checking in with people around you to ensure that you had the impact you intended. You might be surprised to find that, even in the simplest dealings, your impact isn't always received in the way you want, and that's why checking in is so important.

So how do you check in? Simple. You ask what the others got from your words or actions. Listen to what they say. If it's different than your intention, let them know your true intentions, own the miscommunication, and try again.

If you check in with others often enough, you will find that your words, actions, and impact on others become clearer and more aligned with your intentions.

Six

Be Resilient

Be patient and tough; someday this pain will be useful to you.

—Ovid

You've heard "resilience" being tossed around when it comes to leadership, and you might not want to hear it again. But let me tell you: a lot of executives I work with have lost their ability to be resilient. Today, my colleagues and I teach workshops on resilience, yet two decades ago, it wasn't even in our leadership lexicon.

What does resilience mean? Simply put, it means being able to bounce back in the face of adversity. Some of us have lost our bounce. When adversity happens we try to cope, but a lot of leaders don't actually bounce anymore; they work until they break. I see them internalizing their stress, and it comes out in so many destructive ways.

So how can you be more bouncy? You've got to leave things where they land. Take each challenge as it comes; but build a fence around the challenge, and contain it. Don't let it rule your life. Acknowledge it is happening, allow room for you and your team to voice your feelings about it, assess what led you to this place, name the lessons you learned, and then get to work building a new pathway to the future.

It's good to accept responsibility for your part in the challenge, but it's not productive to wallow in self-blame. Be aware, so you don't get caught up in the drama or story of the challenge. Be authentic enough to work through it; then bounce your way out of it.

Seven

Be Honest

Great peacemakers are all people of integrity, of honesty, but humility.

—NELSON MANDELA

H onesty is one of the mighty pillars of all relationships, so it stands to reason that it would be an important quality in a leader whose main charge is to manage relationships among many stakeholders.

Being an honest leader means being able to speak about events, changes, budgets, future hopes, and so on with clarity and truth. By being honest, you are able to form a trusting relationship and, therefore, develop your reputation as a leader with integrity. If your team members or stakeholders are left wondering if some of the information you're giving them may not be reliable, then you may find it difficult to influence them to follow you or to make the decisions that you think are best for all.

Honesty is what builds trust, and trust is the living foundation of all relationships that keeps your team members and stakeholders confident in the job you're doing and the future you are holding as a leader.

Eight

Be Results Oriented

We are what we repeatedly do. Excellence, then,
is not an act, but a habit.

—ARISTOTLE

Being a leader means you are tasked with getting the results your company and your team are aiming for, on time and on budget, while sustaining strong relationships with stakeholders.

But being results oriented is more than just getting to the finish line. It means everything you do each day needs to move the team toward the ultimate goal. Your actions need to show that you can inspire your team members to do their best and that you are able to inspire stakeholders to want what's best for the company, to truly feel that your success is their success.

Thus, results are not just the bottom line on the accounting statement: they're the successful relationships you've built, the savings you've incurred, the trust you've garnered from customers, and the innovation you're modelling for others in your field.

In short, being results oriented means that you are able to build strong, mutually beneficial long-term relationships inside and outside of your team and that you're able to reach your targets along the way.

Nine

Be the First to Laugh
at Yourself

Keep your sense of humor, my friend; if you
don't have a sense of humor it just isn't funny
anymore.

—WAVY GRAVY

Strong leaders are the first to laugh at themselves. This is one of those pieces of wisdom that means much more than it looks like on the surface. Sure, it means being able to poke a little fun at oneself or being self-deprecating and, therefore, humble in the eyes of others. But it also means being able to see your flaws for exactly what they are: a sign of being human.

Too often, I come across leaders who work so incredibly hard to appear perfect. They show signs of deep anxiety by being overly controlling of even the smallest detail. What these leaders can't see is that, somewhere along the way, they've forgotten that being human—making mistakes and being able to laugh at oneself—is the key to being a great leader. It shows others that you don't hold unreal expectations for yourself and that you won't hold them to those unreal expectations, either. It also lets others know that you are fair and approachable and that you know how to live your life with humility and strength of character.

As a leader, it's so important to work on letting go of the façade of perfection. It doesn't exist in nature, and we are natural beings, after all. Give yourself the gift of laughter. It will give you freedom.

Ten

Be a Lifelong Learner

We now accept the fact that learning is a lifelong
process of keeping abreast of change. And the
most pressing task is to teach people how to learn.

—PETER DRUCKER

You're a leader every day, so you're constantly learning on your feet and constantly adapting. Is that enough? Sometimes it can be, but if you're a strong leader, you will also be a lifelong learner. That means that you are a dedicated seeker of knowledge and wisdom, which grow you as a person and a leader.

When you're on the job, learning comes with the territory, so soak it up as much as you can. Keep a list of things you'd really like to learn and the ways you intend to learn them.

Some things may require formal training; what can you do to make room in your schedule? You may be able to learn by picking up a book or two on the subject and accessing wisdom that way. You may choose to interview people who are experts in your field of interest and pick their brains about the way they do things. You may simply watch a TED Talk on the subject matter. Your method of learning is only limited by your imagination.

Go out there. Learn, and bring back your learning to your team.

Eleven

Believe in Transformation

> When we quit thinking primarily about our-
> selves and our own self-preservation, we
> undergo a truly heroic transformation of
> consciousness.

—JOSEPH CAMPBELL

Transformation is more than just a conversation about change. As accomplished coach Alison Van Buuren has taught me, there is a difference between transformational leadership and transactional leadership. Transformational leadership is about working with changes, whether those changes are inevitable or chosen, to create a transformation in yourself and your team that will benefit them in the long term. Transactional leadership is about taking actions to survive a change and move forward without allowing that change to transform and teach you.

It is more than sending your team through a course and having them learn skills that, after a time, get put away on the shelf, along with their course binder. It is more than assessing how to deal with new factors affecting your team. It is about believing that you can engage your team to move from accepting a change to actively creating the environment needed to embrace and develop that change into something workable and worthy of their engagement. That's the transformation piece: moving from accepting a change to reworking it into something that positively changes the team itself.

As a leader, your belief in the value of true transformation will ensure that you commit to what it takes to create long-term adaptation, not just short-term transactional knowledge.

Twelve

Engage Different Stakeholders

Genuine concern for the welfare of others to the point of action is the hallmark of altruism.

—LUKE WESTERMAN

I t's a brand-new day, and, today, leaders need to engage stakeholders in some of their future forecasting processes. Yes, I know. It used to be that you could just make decisions based on what's best for you and your team and then work on making it fly for your stakeholders. Undoubtedly, in some sectors, that may actually still work, but, for the most part, our world is extremely open, thanks to social media and twenty-four-hour access to information on the Internet. Consequently, your stakeholders know just about every decision you make within minutes of making it.

Every one of us is held accountable for our actions everywhere, all the time. Don't kid yourself; you're one YouTube video away from being held accountable for your actions to your stakeholders, too.

I'm not saying this to scare you into doing the right thing. I'm telling you that the world has changed around you, and it's time to walk in an honest, vulnerable, powerful, and strategic way. Invite stakeholders to the table to give you their perspective even if you don't quite agree with them. Be open to giving their views some thought. You'll have to take their perspective into consideration; otherwise, you run the risk of them using social media to shut you down.

What perspectives can you take into consideration when making long-term decisions about your organization? Is there a compromise that could work here? What can you do together to help each other succeed? What is the best way forward?

Thirteen

Be a Critical Thinker

> It is better to debate a question without settling
> it than to settle a question without debating it.
>
> —Joseph Joubert

As a leader, you will be asked on a daily basis to demonstrate your ability to be a critical thinker. Therefore, ensuring you have this skill is fundamental to your leadership.

So what does being a critical thinker entail? It means that you have the ability to think through things in an evaluative and disciplined manner, using observation, history, information gathered from experience, reflection, reasoning, compassion, and intellectual analysis in order to make a decision. In short, do you take into consideration different types of information before taking action? Are you aware of how you gather information and what your personal biases are toward the information you assemble?

Your ability to be a critical thinker gives others confidence that you have strong decision-making qualities. It shows that you are open to many sources of information and will come to a well-thought-out solution for any problems that might arise.

If you need to strengthen your critical-thinking skills, hire a coach who can draw this ability out in you, or hire an expert in critical thinking who can teach you the art of reasoning, questioning, analyzing, and summarizing information quickly. Also, watch those around you whom you believe possess this trait and ask them how they assess their information and how they come to their conclusions about different subject matters. It's a real-time way of learning from someone in your midst who is an expert.

Fourteen

Be Accountable

Accountability breeds response-ability.

—Stephen Covey

We're decades into 360-degree feedback loops and consultation processes, so this should come as no surprise to you. A strong leader needs to be comfortable with being held accountable. In fact, strong leaders need to hold themselves accountable for their own actions.

I've worked with some amazing leaders who understand the importance of being accountable, and they amaze me with the amount of influence they are able to have over their teams and stakeholders because they continually grow themselves.

One leader in particular, who developed his team from a small three-person firm to thousands of employees, is still able, to this day, to inspire every team member just by speaking to him or her one on one. He's tried to retire several times, but his employees have made it clear that they believe he is the heart of the organization and want him to stay.

Why is he so respected? He holds himself accountable to every single employee and asks him or her what he can do better. He is vulnerable and admits when he's wrong. Employees truly feel he cares, and when he asks for feedback, they believe he wants the truth. They love him for it.

This is a leader who goes beyond the degree on his wall or his title. This is a leader who inspires his team because he is the first to hold himself accountable and shows himself a genuine man with a heart that beats with integrity.

Fifteen

Know Thyself

> Self-awareness is not self-centeredness, and
> spirituality is not narcissism. "Know thyself" is
> not a narcissistic pursuit.

—Marianne Williamson

This piece of wisdom is so old it was said to have been inscribed at the temple of Apollo at Delphi. But what does it mean to "know thyself"? More to the point, what does this mean to you as a strong leader?

To know thyself means to dedicate your life to the work it takes to uncover your thoughts, experiences, motivations, strengths, shortcomings, decision-making processes, and goals as well as the deep reasons behind those goals. In short, it is to work consciously on discovering the complexity that makes up *you*.

By discovering the parts that make you who you are, the hope is that you will be truly aware of the behaviour and actions you choose. Knowing thyself also means knowing your impact on others, how your actions affect the people around you.

How this translates to your leadership is that you will become more aware of your strengths, your self-imposed roadblocks, and your effect on others. You will be seen as a person who is working on self-improvement by unraveling your personal story and taking full responsibility for your behaviour. In this way, you are leading yourself in a way that others can admire.

Sixteen

Lead and Follow

In the past, a leader was a boss. Today's leaders must be partners with their people...They no longer can lead solely based on positional power.

—KEN BLANCHARD

Not every situation requires you to jump into the leadership driver's seat. Being a strong leader sometimes means being able to let others lead and making the space to follow. Even when you think you could do it better, you've got to know when to sit back and let others practice their own leadership and do it their own way.

This may be difficult for you. I guarantee you will see different solutions to the problems and you will note some challenges that may come from others' decisions, but that doesn't mean it's necessary for you to take over leadership of the situation. In leadership, you have to trust that, sometimes, the learning that comes from failing is more important than the learning that comes from success. Absolutely, you can coach others to think about their outcomes, but be careful, even then, not to take over or push others into your perspective.

I know I'm asking a lot. You are a strong leader, and, in the end, it may feel like it would be easier if you could just take the wheel. Let go of the controls, and empower others to step up and into their leadership.

Remember that others had to step away and watch you make mistakes until you learned in order for you to become the best leader you could be. So breathe. Just let go. And be there when your team needs you.

Seventeen

Stay Humble

**There is no respect for others without humility
in one's self.**

—Henri-Frédéric Amiel

So you're a strong leader, and you've got drive. That's what got you to where you are. Great job.

Why am I telling you to stay humble when that may not have got you to where you are today? What got you to your leadership position and what will carry you forward are two different things.

Strong leaders need to know when to switch gears and behave in the best way needed at that moment. Staying humble in your leadership position is crucial; after all, you can only lead when others will follow, and they're more likely to follow if they feel you are an unpretentious extension of their team.

You can be aggressive as a humble leader, certainly. You'll want to keep that skill in your cache. It is the lack of arrogance that keeps you humble. As C. S. Lewis said, "True humility is not thinking less of yourself; it's thinking of yourself less."

Eighteen

Take Care of Yourself

Self-preservation is the first law of nature.

—Samuel Butler

I know being a leader can be exhausting, and no one carries the weight of the team as much as you. It's your job as a leader to make it look easy, even when it's hard. You are holding the past success, present actions, and future direction of your team in your hands, so it's vital to keep yourself healthy. It's not just for you; your team members watch your actions and take their direction from your representation of leadership.

Make sure you have a safe way to release the challenges of your work so that you can leave it away from the team. Whether its sports, yoga, knitting, walking, or meditation, do something small every day that gives your body, mind, and soul some solace.

Your team members need you to be at your best so that you can be a positive model for them—especially in stressful times. They look to you for guidance; take care of yourself, and they'll be confident that you can take care of them.

Nineteen

Refrain from Being Defensive

You can't feel compassion if you're defensive.

—Unknown

N one of us likes to feel attacked. Sometimes, when a person attacks our work or behaviour, we come out swinging. We may say or do all manner of nasty things in retaliation. In the moment, it might feel like we're sticking up for ourselves and fighting in self-defence. The reality is it probably looks like we're out of control, defensive, or even in the middle of a childish tantrum.

How should you handle a situation where you feel persecuted? Strong leaders know to take a deep breath and listen without letting ego get in the way. Listen to what the other person is actually saying. Is he or she really mad at you for what you did or didn't do, or is he or she feeling hurt, sad, belittled, or left out? Acknowledge how the other person is truly feeling. This doesn't mean saying "You're right" if you don't mean it; this means saying "I hear you."

Try to see things from the other's perspective. If you can't see that perspective at the moment, no worries; let the person know you will think about his or her words. Walk away. Give it a good think. Come back when you are able to acknowledge the other's perspective and when you can talk about your own without getting into a confrontation.

Bottom line: being defensive can stop you from seeing how others see you and, thus, stop you from growing. It's time to grow.

Twenty

Ask Powerful Questions

To raise new questions, new possibilities, to
regard old problems from a new angle, requires
creative imagination.

—ALBERT EINSTEIN

If you're a leader and you haven't taken any courses on asking powerful open questions, do it. You may already be a seasoned vet who learned this on the job, but if you aren't, then it behooves you to learn how to ask curious and powerful questions so that people feel deeply heard.

It's both an art and a science, and it takes some practice. Good questions will lead people to insights within themselves that they may not have accessed before. Any coach will tell you that powerful questions are probably the biggest tool in our toolbox. Such questions can inspire others to want to take an action, lead them to a new awareness, and even lead people to make transformational changes in their lives.

Asking these questions is the quickest way to make others feel that you care about their opinion; it takes the attention away from you as their "Leader" while it shines a light on them and allows them to feel that they truly matter to you.

Powerful questions can quickly bond people and build relationships of trust, so take the time to learn how to ask powerful questions. For more information on powerful questions, seek advice from a certified coach or access books on coaching and powerful questions. Seminars and videos are also readily available.

Twenty-One

Be Strategically Focused

The biggest risk is not taking any risk.

—MARK ZUCKERBERG

Being strategically focused is a key component of being a good leader. So what does strategic focus, or strategic thinking, mean? It means that you have developed the ability to think in a critical manner and are able to see insights and opportunities that could benefit your team. Moreover, you are focused on innovation and methods of change that could be adapted beneficially for your team, and you implement them where it makes sense.

Strategic thinkers run this insight and opportunity matrix like a platform in the background of their work. Every experience and interaction is looped through your strategic-thinking mind in order to assess whether or not your team could benefit from it.

You know how you know you're a strategic thinker? You look at an article on the newsstands and you think, "We can benefit from that." You see something on the news and think, "We can do that." You hear something your team member says and you think, "We can implement that." That's strategic thinking.

It goes without saying that you have to balance strategic thinking with strategic action, so it doesn't mean taking action on every opportunity.

You need to temper a new strategy against past failures and successes and to measure the opportunity with the wisdom or insight of the past and the vision of the future.

Twenty-Two

Be Optimistic

Optimism is the foundation of courage.

—ELEANOR ROOSEVELT

One trait I've found to be key to all strong leaders is the ability to stay optimistic even in the most difficult moments. Whether they be civil rights leaders, environmental activists, or Fortune 500 CEOs, leaders who stay strong through hardships are the ones who can hold an optimistic vision through it all.

Being optimistic simply means you honour the reasons why you chose this path; you inspire your team to continue to reach for the goal; you stay open to learning and flowing as new, innovative methods come along; and you remain optimistic to the possibility of a successful outcome.

The ultimate goal may end up being different than you intended—even your reasons for continuing down your path may change—but remaining optimistic, even when others aren't, may be the crucial factor needed for you and your team to get to the end.

Twenty-Three

Be Aware of Your Challenges

Know yourself to improve yourself.

—AUGUSTE COMTE

I t's not easy to focus on your shortcomings. As a leader, you're in a position where you need to constantly grow in order to hold your value to your group. This means looking with an honest eye at your strengths and also at the places where you may need to improve.

So how do you do this? Start with asking for feedback formally or informally. Seek input from the people in your team who represent diverse voices, not just from the ones who might be your fans.

It would be easy to play it safe by asking only the people who like you to give you feedback, but you're working toward being a stronger leader. It's time to model courageous leadership by being open to those who will give you their honest perspective in order to aid your growth and maturity.

Once you get your feedback, read it carefully. It's easy to skim through the critical stuff and look for the positive, but I'm asking you to be strong and work through your discomfort. All feedback is important for your personal leadership development.

See if you agree with the feedback you've been given. Take the positive to heart, and build on it. If you disagree with the feedback, what are your reasons? Be clear that you're not just disagreeing because you don't want to hear anything negative. Learning is uncomfortable; get comfortable with it. If receiving honest feedback is hard for you, hire a coach and work through it. It's important.

Twenty-Four

Hold Your Own Personal Leadership Vision

Self-leadership is the precursor to effectively leading others.

—Reed B. Markham

When leaders holds their own personal vision for leadership, they show others that they are moving in a positive intentional direction. If you are holding a vision for your team, it's important to hold it for yourself as well so that you know where you're headed.

Start by assessing where you are now. Look at the kind of leader you are and where you'd like to be in three months, six months, and one year. Build a plan for how you're going to get there. Be realistic. Get a coach to help you plan out your strategy, or go it alone and put some action words in your plan.

What will you do today, next week, and every week to move toward your goal? Can you learn by reading a book, taking a course, or going to a conference? Can you learn by speaking with someone whom you admire and asking how he or she got to be the type of leader you want to be?

Build a time line so that you can assess if you're on the right track. Stop and celebrate the milestones, whether they are a book read or a conference done. Share your personal leadership vision with others so they can support you and help you grow along the way by holding you accountable.

Twenty-Five

Ask for Honest Feedback

We all need people who give us feedback.
That's how we improve.

—BILL GATES

We all know how hard it can be to receive honest feedback. So why is it important to do it? Feedback is a crucial tool for good leaders to grow into strong leaders. Asking for honest feedback and being able to receive it show others that you are open to learning and to improving your leadership capacity.

How can you lead if you're not open? You'd be hard-pressed to find followers if you were closed to learning about yourself and the way you lead others. It's true that, in the world of work, you'll sometimes find leaders who are not open to learning, but those days are coming to an end.

It is a growing norm to be held accountable as a leader not only for the way you lead but for the way you are "seen" to lead. The people whom you lead need to see that you have the best intentions when you make decisions. They need to feel confident that you are not running a personal agenda but are looking out for the whole team. After all, it's your team that you're asking to follow you into the unknown; ask them for feedback, and find out how you're doing at being their leader.

Get a 360-degree feedback tool, and choose people to participate who like you—and some folks who don't. Be honest. Be open. Learn from the people you depend on and who depend on you.

Twenty-Six

Develop a Plan from Feedback Received

Planning is bringing the future into the present
so that you can do something about it now.

—ALAN LAKEIN

So you've gone out and asked for feedback, and you've got all sorts of juicy bits of information both good and bad. Congratulations. As a colleague of mine often says, it's "another freaking learning opportunity." Now what do you do with it? Well, it's time to put the feedback to good use.

Look at the information you've gathered with an open mind and a critical eye. What do you see? Where is there consistency? What things surprised you? What aspects were positive? Where could you improve?

Now take a minute to assess your feelings (yes, I said "feelings") about how others see you. This is an important process for growing your EQ. What feelings come up? Where are these coming from? What lesson do you need to learn from those feelings?

Once you've read and felt your way through the information, it's time to acknowledge it, sort it, and develop a plan. Look at one or two areas that you would like to improve. Don't try to change all of it. Choose wisely what will give you the most leverage in your leadership at that moment.

Decide what achievable actions you're willing to take to make improvements in these areas. Set a time frame for yourself so that you can gauge whether or not you're on the right track. Add markers to alert you when you've reached small goals. You're on your way.

Twenty-Seven

Have a Sense of Humour

> You can't really be strong until you see a funny
> side to things.
>
> —Ken Kesey

We've all had bosses who couldn't laugh at themselves and took every task as seriously as a heart attack. How fun was it to work for them? Chances are not much fun at all.

Today's work culture needs you to show up as a fully functional human being, not just as a "Leader." People want to know you have a sense of humour and can laugh at yourself when you make a mistake. Can you do that?

They want to know that you are fallible (like them) and that when mistakes are made, you learn from them instead of denying the mistake, shaming yourself, or giving up. Having a sense of humour teaches others that you will allow them to make mistakes because you understand that this is sometimes the most powerful way of learning.

Sharing our mistakes, and even a laugh, is the shortest way to build trust between two human beings, so stop taking yourself so seriously. Lead from the funny bone and from your heart rather than from the fear that you need to be perfect all the time. Perfection doesn't exist, so it's best to leave that behind and model being a conscious leader.

Twenty-Eight

Be Vulnerable

Vulnerability is about showing up and being
seen. It's tough to do that when we're terrified
about what people might see or think.

—Brené Brown

Before you bypass this one, stop for a moment, and read on. What does it mean to be vulnerable? It doesn't mean to allow others to walk all over you or to hurt you because you aren't willing to defend yourself. To be vulnerable as a leader simply means to allow yourself to be seen. To show yourself to be present in your own life and able to share when you have made a mistake or when you have changed your mind. In short, it means not hiding from your human capacity.

Being a vulnerable leader takes courage. It takes strength. Ask Brené Brown, who literally wrote the book on it. According to Brené, vulnerability is nonnegotiable in business. You can't opt out of it. To be a leader, you have to put yourself out there and try things in an entrepreneurial way, and that means opening yourself up to vulnerability. It's part and parcel of leadership, so you'd be wise to learn to own it sooner rather than later.

Up until now, we haven't been taught to allow ourselves the room to be vulnerable in our leadership position because it hasn't been valued in past generations. Yet, when we look back at leaders in past generations, we see a big gap in emotional intelligence. The EQ piece is now a must for leaders, and that includes the ability to be vulnerable. If you're still wondering what it means, I encourage you to pick up one of Brené Brown's books. It just may change your life.

Twenty-Nine

Be a Visionary

The visionary starts with a clean sheet of paper and reimagines the world.

—MALCOLM GLADWELL

Being a visionary is a foundational pillar of great leadership. It is the ability to see a possible future with courage and wisdom while holding the present in capable hands. It is about being a pioneer in order to grow the team toward the best outcome.

Visionary leaders consult with other stakeholders in order to assess and reassess the best plan of action, but they must be able to hold to the vision and work toward it as long as that vision is still in the best interest of the whole.

One such visionary is the Dalai Lama. Known for his peace activism and his nonviolent struggle for the liberation of his homeland in Tibet, Tenzin Gyatso (Dalia Lama) holds his vision of peace even in the face of extremely aggressive action against his people. I once had the good fortune of meeting his brother, Tenzin Choegyal, and hearing him speak. He reminded our small group that the Dalai Lama is no more or less than any other human. What makes him remarkable in the eyes of others is that he is able to sustain, day in and day out, the vision that peace is essential to solving all global issues and that it is ever attainable. When you are this kind of a visionary, you inspire the world.

Thirty

Be Well Rounded

> You have to be a well-rounded leader...you have to be incredibly tough-minded about standards of performance, but you also have to be incredibly tenderhearted with the people you're working with.
>
> —Douglas Conant

Today's leaders need to be innovative, inspiring, and well rounded. What does that mean? It means that Generation X and the upcoming Millennial's value a leader who has a strong educational background and valuable work experience as well as a worldly perspective derived from fulfilling personal-life experiences. They also value leaders who are altruistic and have made a difference by volunteering or working to better a community or culture in need.

Leaders are scrutinized for leadership in and out of the office. Jeff Skoll, the president of eBay, is widely known for giving about half of his income to organizations that help benefit society in the fields of health, food security, education, environment, and more. Other leaders, such as President Jimmy Carter, have an extraordinary track record for their volunteerism with organizations, such as Habitat for Humanity.

It's crucial—now more than ever—to continue to grow yourself as a well-rounded leader and give back in whatever way you can. We've talked about large-scale giving, but on a small scale, you could use a car share, ride your bike to work, or give to the local food bank. It's up to you to determine what is within your ability, but note that this trend toward altruism is not going anywhere soon. Being well rounded is the new mark of a strong leader; it shows that you have integrity and will care as much for your team and your company as you do for your community.

Thirty-One

Start Where You Are

Just where you are—that's the place to start!

—PEMA CHODRON

So you're a leader, and things aren't going as well as you'd like. What do you do? As Pema Chodron wrote, start where you are (with whomever is in front of you).

Wherever you and your team are at this moment is a good place to begin to turn the tide. Start by making some basic assessments. Assess yourself as a leader. This can mean having a 360-degree feedback done and allowing different types of people on your team to give you honest feedback. It might mean getting a coach to help direct you in your leadership journey. Second, assess your team. Do they have the resources, tools, and materials that they need to get their job done? Are they clear about what their roles are and what is expected of them? Does each individual have the capacity, attitude, desire, skills, and knowledge to do his or her work? Does the culture you work in promote positive communication and growth? You can find out by asking questions, such as: "Do you have all the resources you need?" "Do you feel prepared for this task?" "Is there anything else you need to meet your deadline?"

Assess how you're showing up for others and whether or not you are having the impact you want on your team. Work with your team to take action toward making constructive changes. Start exactly where you are, and lead your team to a healthier way of being. There's no time like the present.

Thirty-Two

Don't Be Afraid to Try Something New

> When I dare to be powerful, to use my strength
> in the service of my vision, then it becomes less
> and less important whether I am afraid.

—AUDRE LORDE

So you're in the midst of holding your team together, and you're really in the muck, getting things done as fast and efficiently as possible. Wonderful. Now here I am inviting you to try new things on top of your already burdened workload. What? It's true. Here's why: the need for new energy is never more pertinent than when your team has got into the habit of working at the level of *status quo* (which, most often, is a high level of stress).

Your team needs inspiration, and the easiest way to do that is to shake it up right where you are. Try something new. It doesn't have to be big or costly. A mini check-in is a good place to start. I'm not trying to get touchy feely with you; I'm trying to help you see that your team is made up of people, not instruments.

Stay connected, and give people a sense of community again. Check in with your team members, and give them room to check in with each other—whether you do it at a meeting or a social event. Research shows that where there is a sense of community, people are more likely to go out of their way for others and less likely to do things to hurt them. Connect your team.

What about you? I encourage you to, once in a while, try something positive that you would never try normally. A new type of food, a new adventure, or a type of movie you wouldn't normally watch. These small actions keep you malleable and open and strong as a leader.

Thirty-Three

Take the Time to Reflect

**Since everything is a reflection of our minds...
everything can be changed by our minds.**

—BUDDHA

Amid all the busyness that we call life, leaders need to put down the mantle of leadership and just reflect. It's only in this reflection that we can see what has happened and what has brought us to this moment. In reflection, we are able to take the time to learn about our reactions to events that occurred and to assess whether or not we would handle them differently now.

All the answers to our internal questions lie in being able to stop and reflect. Through this one act, we are better able to see our responsibility for the success and failures of our team. Without it, we are simply moving from predicament to predicament, and we lack the insight to learn and grow from each challenge.

Create a habit of reflection each day by going on quiet walks, journaling, rowing, or meditating, for example. Strong leaders not only take the down time needed to reflect; they also encourage reflection in the group by deconstructing events together and picking out the golden threads of learning.

Thirty-Four

Allow Room for Mistakes

A man must be big enough to admit his mistakes, smart enough to profit from them, and strong enough to correct them.

—JOHN C. MAXWELL

You're a leader, and you do your best to lead with confidence, care, and openness. As a leader, you will make mistakes. No problem. Leadership is learning, so it's vital that you get used to accepting the mistakes and the losses without making a magnificent drama out of it.

When others make mistakes, it's your turn to remember that it's an opportunity for learning. Refrain from being overly critical, and watch the language you use. You want to deepen the learning for your team members and create new pathways to future solutions, so be careful not to alienate or shame them.

As Dr. Peter A. Cooperrider, the father of appreciative inquiry, says, "Words create worlds." Use your words wisely, and coach others to grow from their mistakes. Be good to yourself as well, and refrain from beating yourself up. Mourn the mistake; assess the options you have for moving forward; rebuild, learn, and move on.

Thirty-Five

Create an Inspiring Space

Happiness is not a matter of intensity, but of balance, order, rhythm, and harmony.

—Thomas Merton

Create a healthy *physical* space for all your team members. Your office, warehouse, headquarters...wherever it is your team works is vital to creating the culture of your company and dictating the morale for your team members.

Companies like Google, Lego, Red Bull, AOL, Facebook, and YouTube know that a healthy space that inspires equates to higher productivity over time. Their use of fun architecture, good lighting, colourful details, and creatively designed space all add up to high employee satisfaction.

So what does your physical environment say about you and your team? Is it in line with your cultural values? Does it show that you are putting your team first on your list of priorities?

Obviously, we can't always have the space we want, but what small steps can you take to create a calm, inspiring, healthy, safe, and inviting place for your team members and stakeholders? Can you seek guidance from your team members about what they would like to see in the space to help them feel more connected to each other and to their work? What small action are you and your team willing to take to create a work environment that reflects your values, culture, and tradition?

Thirty-Six

Name the Elephant
in the Room

You can choose courage, or you can choose comfort, but you cannot choose both.

—BRENE BROWN

It's not easy being in a state of discomfort, and, goodness knows, I don't want to tell you to actively seek it out. But the reality is that, as a leader, you will need to get comfortable with discomfort, especially where relationships within your team are concerned.

It's an important part of your job to see clearly when there is a fracture in your team, and it's your task to name it. You're responsible for the health of your team, so if you see something brewing into a conflict, it's your job to name the elephant in the room and allow the space for your people to deal with it the best way they can.

I know what you might be thinking: if I name it, I could potentially open a can of worms. Better a can of worms now than a serious crisis within the team later.

If you think you're no good at conflict and you need help, don't be afraid to ask for it. There are wonderful coaches and consultants out there who can help you gain the skills you need to deal with breakdowns in the team environment, or they can simply step in, mediate, and give you time to get confident. Whichever way you choose, you'll need to learn to deal with issues, head on, in their infancy before they become a real challenge to the whole team. Get comfortable naming the elephant, and do it early.

Thirty-Seven

Lead from Within, Beside, Behind, and In Front

> When someone is walking beside us, we have more courage to walk into the unknown and to risk the dark and messy places in our journey.

— Henry Kimsey-House

Two wise people, Henry and Karen Kimsey-House, put leadership into one succinct, continually evolving statement that captures the essence of being a leader. A leader leads from within, sometimes beside, sometimes behind, and sometimes in front.

Simply put, this means that you need to be aware of yourself as a leader (within), your motivation, and the impact you want to have on others. It also means, sometimes, leading alongside others as an equal. At times, you need to know when to take the back seat and allow others to take the wheel. Last, it means standing fully in your leadership power and leading your team from the front.

Being a strong leader means you can move from position to position, sometimes minute by minute. Noticing where you're leading from and being mindful of each position of leadership you choose bring you to a more conscious form of leadership. The more conscious you are, the more aware you'll become of your impact and the more you can direct that impact to a favourable ending.

Henry and Karen, as wise as they are, continue to grow and change this statement with the help of thousands of other coaches in our community. The next time you hear about this statement, it could look very different because they believe that leadership never stops evolving.

Thirty-Eight

Bridge Generations

Every generation revolts against its fathers and
makes friends with its grandfathers.

—LEWIS MUMFORD

Whether you are a baby boomer, Generation X, or millennial leader, you need to be able to bridge the gap of all generations working in your team. That means getting up to speed on what gifts and challenges each generation brings, understanding the context in which they have lived their lives, and, thus, valuing their experiences and mind-set.

Once you learn about and respect each generation, you will gain more empathy for their decision-making processes and value their input in the team rather than judge them against the criteria of your own generation.

Bridging the generations is a great way to build a diverse team and to teach others how to relate to different age groups around them. Having different age groups within your team also helps to create trust among stakeholders who want to see themselves (or the possibility of themselves) reflected in the dynamics of your organizational culture.

Seek out books on the generation gap, and gain insight by having open-minded conversations with others outside of your generation. Ask questions to garner their perspective on things you may take for granted, such as voting, citizenship, driving a car, and using a computer. Ask about their lives and their paths to where they are now.

Learn to listen with an open heart and open mind, and share your perspective so that they understand your generation as well.

Thirty-Nine

Don't Use Fear to Motivate

> The enemy is fear. We think it is hate,
> but it is fear.

—MAHATMA GANDHI

So we know theoretically that it's a bad idea to use fear as a long-term motivator. But why is that? Well, let's break it down.

It's true that fear has proven to work in leadership in a lot of different scenarios throughout history, but we've learned over time that fear is not a sustainable way to get people to follow. Sometimes, however, we can be leading from fear and not even realize it. If you find that you're the type of leader who is constantly reminding people about time crunches, deadlines, and bottom lines, you may actually be leading from fear.

Of course, some environments, like surgical rooms and stock-market floors, are, by their very nature, pressurized; so we're not talking about those places (though it's still a good idea to see if you can manage people in those situations with inspiration rather than fear).

People feel intimidated, stressed out, and fearful when their leader or person they report to creates an environment of anxiety in order to function. I've come across this time and again, and often the leaders tell me that they need to do this to "motivate" the team to get the work done. They blame it on the stressful work environment, but they often aren't able to see that they themselves are actually the cause of unnecessary stress for their team members.

Check it out with your team members. Find out if you're leading by fear.

Forty

Mark Important Traditions

Without our traditions...the community would lose its grounding.

—FIDDLER ON THE ROOF

Strong leaders understand the very important need to celebrate milestones.

We, as humans, celebrate everything, including births, graduations, weddings, birthdays, retirements, and even death. Rituals around certain occasions act as initiations for individuals or bring closure regarding the past. We gather together to mark grief or loss and to support each other in a new future.

As a leader, it's important to take the time with your group to mark an occasion, whether you deem it negative or positive. Making room for others to share their feelings gives them an opportunity to be heard, hear others, and move into a more positive future.

Take the time to celebrate events that are important to your team. Show that you care for the whole of their being, not just the part that shows up to work. Whether you are celebrating a birthday with doughnuts or marking an important company change with an impromptu burning of old binders, a celebration doesn't have to be costly to be effective. What's important is that you give space for the members of your group to share their feelings and feel heard and accepted by all.

Forty-One

Know When to Coach and When to Direct

In business, we have to be both coaches and managers. To lead effectively, we need to know when to wear which hat.

—HOLLY GREEN

Sometimes, as a leader, you will have the opportunity and privilege of coaching others so that they may grow into their own personal leadership strengths. When you have the time and commitment to do this, you are giving your team members the gift of empowerment. When they have space to make mistakes, they know that you've got their backs, and they can continue to grow in confidence and strength. Coaching them means asking them powerful open-ended questions that inspire them to look within for answers and to come up with new ways of doing things that yield positive results.

Sometimes, however, as a leader, you will need to direct your team members into action. This might happen during an emergency or a crisis; it might even happen when there is a serious time crunch and actions need to be taken to ensure things move forward. Strong leaders prepare their staff for direction or coaching by practicing both at different times so that team members learn to be comfortable with both forms of leadership. It's important that you, as a leader, know when it's the right time to coach and when it's the right time to direct and that you know what your reasons are for doing either in a given situation. Both will be of great benefit to your team if used correctly.

Forty-Two

Check In Often

The biggest communication problem is we do
not listen to understand. We listen to reply.

—UNKNOWN

D o you know how leaders know they're on the right track? Simple. They check in with their team often. Sure, you may be a good leader if you utilize a 360-degree feedback tool once a year, but it's more than just getting feedback for your overall leadership. It's about checking in with people daily and learning what your impact is on them (thus developing trust). What did they hear from what you just said in the meeting? Are they aligned with your vision? Do they even understand it? What questions do people have about the process you are asking them to undertake? What can you do to make your requests and your information more clear?

As my executive clients have learned after years in the leadership world, when they want to know how a person feels about what's going on, they simply ask.

Remember this: asking a person directly (rather than going through others or listening to rumours and gossip) is the only way to get accurate information. If people are comfortable with you, they will tell you their perspectives honestly. If they aren't comfortable enough to be honest, then that, too, is information you can use to work on creating a more trusting relationship.

Forty-Three

Give Room for Other Opinions

> The greatest deception men suffer is from their own opinions.
>
> —LEONARDO DA VINCI

No leader is an island, and that's especially true if you want to lead a successful team. By its very nature, the word "team" implies a group of people. What better way to lead a group of people than by listening for their wisdom and making them feel heard?

Being a strong leader means allowing room for other people's opinions and assessing the viability of their perspective against the outcome of your decisions. Or, as my UK friends say, "Give it a good think." You may, in the end, decide to go with your own line of thinking, but giving it a good think is a worthy exercise because it shows you value others' opinions and you're open to learning.

Allowing room for other opinions also keeps you relevant and in touch with the pulse of what's going on around you. It can be easy to get caught up in the action of meeting a goal…so much so that we forget that a goal can be a moving target and that we need to remain open to adapting to changes that are happening around us.

Trust your team to keep you grounded with their opinions. Trust yourself to make the decisions that need to be made.

Forty-Four

Develop Leadership Capacity in Others

> Leaders don't create followers; they create more leaders.

> —Tom Peters

It's as simple as the quote above. Your tasks as a leader are to lead and, also, to develop other leaders from your fold. I can't tell you how many times I've been hired to find out why employees are leaving a particular department or site only to find out the issue lies with a leader who wasn't willing to build leadership capacity in others. Worse still is when I come across a leader who purposefully puts up roadblocks to others' success. Good, strong employees end up leaving this type of situation because they feel they have no room to grow, and they are not being supported to succeed by the very leader they work under.

Why would leaders behave in this way? It may be personal leadership insecurity, fear of losing their job, fear of being "found out" as an incapable leader (imposter syndrome), jealousy, or just outright sociopathic behaviour. There are many reasons. What I know is that confident, strong leaders have no problems building the leadership capacity of others around them even if it means that they will eventually lose their team members because the members become leaders themselves. People are more likely to want to work for such a leader, and you're more likely to attract the best because you will have built a reputation for creating strong leaders in the world.

Forty-Five

Don't Be Afraid of Conflict

Peace is not the absence of conflict but the ability to cope with it.

—Dorothy Thomas

You'd be surprised how often I come across a leader who is afraid of conflict. I often wonder how he or she got to a place of leadership without this crucial skill. Conflict is the birthplace of creativity and, some would even say, life. Conflict is vastly important because it is the breeding ground for new ideas, shared values, growth, and inspiration.

Good news for leaders: being comfortable with conflict is a skill you can learn. First, do an internal check about what it is that makes you uncomfortable with conflict. What part of it upsets you most? It's important to know what it is you might be avoiding.

As a leader, you've got to learn to move through conflict because you'll be dealing with it a lot. Don't get caught up in each person's story; stay as neutral as you can, and focus on the behaviours or the event, not just on the people involved. Deal with the conflict early and directly by addressing it in real time. Define with your team what you agree to be acceptable behaviour in the workplace, and stick to those agreements. Try to bring the players involved in the conflict together to work on a resolution, and if you can't do that, then it's time to bring in an expert.

You don't need to get involved personally in the drama of the conflict; you just have to be confident enough to acknowledge it early on and to help your team members come up with their own solutions.

Forty-Six

Understand That Things Can Always Go Wrong

Sometimes when things are falling apart, they may actually be falling into place.

—UNKNOWN

Do you ever notice that we make wonderful plans for our lives and yet, no matter how hard we try, those plans sometimes can't prepare us for the reality? It happens a lot; it's called life.

So why is it that we are absolutely shocked when things don't go as we planned? It's all about assumptions. We build our plans, and we assume that things are going to go smoothly; and when things vary from the plan, we become disappointed, angry, sad, frustrated, and anxious and may even blame others.

We lose our ability to cope when we've built up our expectations to the degree that any small change throws us off. It's our job, then, as leaders to ensure that we remain flexible and roll with the punches. We need to understand that sometimes—nay, often—things won't go our way, and when they don't, we need to remember that we are in the business of modelling resilience for our team.

Acknowledge to yourself and your team that things aren't going as expected. Allow room for upset; then move into assessing the situation.

Do a quick forensic audit of what got your team here, and then focus on what you have learned and what will get your team to the next stage. Remember that just because things go wrong doesn't mean there isn't great learning to be had. Stay flexible and open; and, above all, teach it to your team.

Forty-Seven

Don't Tolerate Prejudice

> Do you know what we call opinion in the
> absence of evidence? We call it prejudice.

—Michael Crichton

Prejudice is a subtle and dangerous way to erode morale in the best of teams. I'm not just speaking about the obvious prejudgments of race, gender, age, and sexual orientation. There is no room for that in any team. I'm speaking about the type of prejudice that often gets passed off as fact. You know the kind: where we talk about the influx of a certain people who are taking over our jobs or about not being able to understand taxi drivers' accents and how "they" should learn to speak English better.

These prejudices are shared almost daily in social situations, and it's not enough to ignore them or to say to yourself that the person who is saying it is just rude and unenlightened. This behavior is unacceptable in the workplace. As a leader, it is your job to grow your team and make it safe for everyone to feel comfortable; therefore, you must set a clear boundary here.

One of my executive clients in a culturally diverse organization simply asks team members to say out loud the word "uncomfortable" when a statement is made that makes them feel hurt or awkward. This worked well in their group to raise the consciousness of the group and make individuals aware of prejudices they may not know they harbour, and it became a light, easy way to teach and learn in real time.

Forty-Eight

See Beyond Victim, Villain, and Hero

> If you have not been a villain at a certain point in time, you will never be a hero. And the day you are a hero, you may become a villain the next day.

—CARLOS GHOSN

It's important to remove yourself from the day-to-day fray of workplace relationships in order for you to bring more wisdom and clarity into any situation. It may be hard, but it's not impossible; and it's never more needed than when there is a conflict in your team environment.

You may already recognize that most people in a conflict situation refer to themselves as either victims or heroes; some, on rare occasions, may even be able to see themselves as villains. We first heard this language in the book *Nonviolent Communication* by Marshall B. Rosenburg, where we learned that it is possible to be all three of these in one incident. Team members may feel victimized and then stand up for themselves in unskillful ways that verge on bullying; they may think they are being heroes when they may have actually devolved into being villains.

As a leader, it's up to you to take a higher perspective and stay clear of buying into one side or another. You may need to bring the parties together for a conversation; it may also be necessary to bring in a conflict coach or a union representative to assess the best way to heal the situation. This doesn't mean you get to bow out and show no interest; you still need to acknowledge that there is an issue and clearly state your desire to resolve it in the best way possible. The key is to refrain from getting involved in a "he-said, she-said" game of victim, villain, and hero and to move into solutions.

Forty-Nine

Only Ask of Others What You Are Willing to Do Yourself

It is not fair to ask of others what you are not
willing to do yourself.

—Eleanor Roosevelt

In 2014 the chief executive of a large Liverpool hospital took part in a "change day," where she traded her desk job for mops and teamed up with the cleaners for the day.

Many organizations have taken part in this type of event and have found it extremely successful because it builds morale, creates stronger relationships, gives executives an opportunity to listen to the staff's ideas and concerns, and shows executives what these jobs really entail.

You don't have to wait to unveil a formal event in order to connect with your own team. You can practice, in the moment, your willingness to do what you ask of others. Team members want to see that their leaders are committed and aren't above getting their hands dirty—whether that means leaders moving garbage out of the building or staying late with their team members in order to meet a deadline. They want to see that you understand what it takes to get the job done and that when you say a deadline is important, you will be there to help them meet it.

Be the leader who is willing to roll up your sleeves and work alongside your team. Be the one whom they trust.

Fifty

Seek to Understand Before Being Understood

Wise men don't judge: they seek to understand

—WEI WU WEI

Sometimes, we can't help ourselves; we let ourselves get caught up in being right. We pick a perspective, and we fight for that perspective against anyone who has a different view. In conflict management, this isn't the smartest way to win a battle. Likewise, in leadership, it's the fastest way to shut down communication.

If you want to influence others to see your point of view, you've got to truly see their perspective first. This means spending time asking curious questions, really trying to unravel why they believe what they believe. When you can truly get to a point where you can see their perspective, begin by acknowledging them and check in to see if you understand them. Once they feel heard, others will be more willing to hear you. Remain calm, and share your perspective in a respectful way that doesn't belittle or shame the other person.

Most of all, be honest and authentic; don't try to fake it. People are wonderfully intuitive, so you need to truly be seeking to understand them—not just trying to get enough ammo to win a fight.

Be curious, humble, and kind when you seek to understand. Allow room to learn something new. Acknowledge others authentically for what they're bringing to the table. Share your perspective with humility and grace. Learn on.

Fifty-One

Communicate Well

The art of communication is the language of leadership.

—James Humes

Leaders come in all sorts of strengths. Some leaders are charismatic, and some are introverted. Some are passionate, and some are calculating. What all strong leaders share is the ability to communicate well with those around them. This is vital in leadership because you are influencing others to follow you, and you do that through your words and deeds. If you cannot communicate your vision, purpose, and goals with others in a way that they can hear it, then it is difficult for those around you—in your workplace, church, or home—to willingly follow you.

A high value is placed on how our leaders communicate through spoken and written words. Think of the leaders in your community and in the world today. Most, if not all, have an ability to reach out and win strangers over to their perspective simply by being strong communicators. Mahatma Gandhi, Martin Luther King Jr., both Canadian prime ministers Pierre and Justin Trudeau, Sir Winston Churchill, Oprah, and Richard Branson are just a few leaders who mastered the art of communication as a foundation of their leadership.

It's important, therefore, to continue to work on your written and verbal communication skills. Read as much as you can to improve your language proficiency; watch videos of the orators that you hold in high esteem; and break down the attributes that you would like to work on. Practice as much as possible.

Fifty-Two

Tell a Damn Good Story

To hell with facts! We need stories!

—Ken Kesey

The best leaders I've ever witnessed in action have the gift of gab. I've been in tough situations that seemed impossible to overcome and have watched a leader win people over through the simple act of telling one damn good story.

It's ancient technology to be certain, and it works extremely well because we as humans have been designed to relate to a good story. It's the way we market (commercials); it's the way we sell movies; it's the way we influence one another; and it's the way we share our values with our children. Being able to tell a story is the fastest way to create trust in a room full of strangers.

So do you have the gift of gab? Here's how you can build up your ability as a storyteller. Watch people tell stories to determine whose style you like. What is it about their storytelling that you like? What kept you engaged? How long did they speak? Did they have a point to their story? Did they stick to the point?

Research online, or go to the bookstore for resources about storytelling. Practice as much as possible in both formal and informal settings.

Hire a storytelling expert to help you, or join a toastmasters group to learn how to speak eloquently, make concise points, and hold your audience.

Don't underestimate this skill; it's one you can benefit from for the rest of your life.

Fifty-Three

Create a Positive Environment

> Positive anything is better than negative
> nothing.

—ELBERT HUBBARD

I know this goes without saying, but like everything else in leadership, it shouldn't be taken for granted. We are living in an age where "faster," "more," and "now" are the norm. We are bombarded with messages that we are not enough, and this can lead to debilitating negative self-talk. In light of all of this, we sometimes lose our sense of calm and peace. As a leader, therefore, it's important to provide an environment that is as positive, calm, and peaceful as possible in order for your team members to do their best work.

It doesn't matter if you're in a time crunch situation every day or if you're saving lives; the way you fashion your environment will either give your team members a sense of peace or make them feel more anxious.

You can model professional composure and good leadership skills by being positive and supportive to your team members. Don't be caught up in being "busy." Work smart, and teach others how to do the same. Create a positive environment that values kindness, peace, teamwork, and shared responsibility and that leaves no room for drama.

Remember that *you* lead the environment, so take stock of how things are going in your world and make the changes necessary to ensure your workplace is a soft place for your team to land.

Fifty-Four

Gather a Team with Diverse Perspectives

> You have to get along with people, but you also have to recognize that the strength of a team is different people with different perspectives and different personalities.
>
> —STEVE CASE

Most of the time, when we look at our friends, we see that they are very much like us. They think the same things, are part of the same economic demographic, and hold the same morals and ethics as we do. In short, we attract people who have the same values as we do.

In leadership, however, we need to do something that may seem counterintuitive. Strong leaders gather a team with different perspectives. I'm not suggesting creating a team where everyone disagrees on every topic. On the contrary, begin by gathering people who hold the same basic values, such as honesty, integrity, and respect. Personal values should match the direction your company is going.

From there, your team's makeup should reflect different experiences, ages, gender, cultural understanding, and points of view. The more diverse the team members, the better for your stakeholders because they represent a greater portion of the world's view.

The trick is to be a strong-enough leader to lead this type of diversity. That's the duty and challenge a strong leader takes on. Don't be afraid of the conflict that comes up with a diverse team. This is the time to teach your team how to communicate with each other in a way that builds on each other's diversity. Keep in mind that the best solutions will come from seeing things through many eyes.

Fifty-Five

Don't Allow Bullying

I find it's usually the bullies who are the most
insecure.

—TOM FELTON

"Bullying" is an important word in our children's vernacular; even at their young ages, they have most likely already encountered it as victims or bystanders. Bullying doesn't just happen on the playground; it's important for leaders to remember that bullying happens in our workplaces as well.

Bullying can be subtle, as in the telling of off-colour jokes that might be racist in nature. It can also be more sinister, as in a team member threatening a fellow coworker with violence or a manager intimidating an employee with the potential loss of work.

A strong leader will not allow a culture of bullying even in its smallest form. It's your task to create and sustain a healthy antibullying environment where all your team members feel free to be their strongest selves.

If you aren't confident enough at this point in your leadership to deal with bullying, get some external help. Don't wait until you have the skills; your inability to deal with bullies might cause someone to get hurt or lose his or her job. Get an expert to help you and your team clear the air, deal with any underlying issues, seek advice from your union or lawyers if need be, and strengthen the environment by making it safe for all people.

Remember that it's much easier to deal with the spark of conflict or bullying than the burning fire that could result from inaction.

Fifty-Six

Create Safety

If we cannot now end our differences, at least
we can help make the world safe for diversity.

—JOHN F. KENNEDY

Y ou may think you create safety in your work environment, but you
may not be able to see the whole picture.

Let's start by defining "safety." In this case, safety means the ability
for a team member to have a voice in the group and feel safe in sharing
that voice. Some leaders feel that the job of the group is to go along with
the leader and get things done. That's not leadership; that's a dictator-
ship, and it doesn't allow individuals to feel safe in bringing up alternative
perspectives.

Strong leaders aren't afraid of their team members voicing their opinions even if they're different from their own. In fact, a resilient leader
encourages others to have a voice and offers security so that all team
members feel they will be supported to speak up. Safety also means not
tolerating slander or abuse when a team member voices an unpopular
opinion.

The best way to create this kind of environment is to model it for your
team. When someone speaks up with a different opinion, acknowledge
the courage that it takes to do so. Clarify his or her statement so that it's

clear that you understand what he or she is saying. And strive to speak to the issue honestly.

The overlying theme here is respect. Speak with respect; listen with respect; and allow everyone to walk away feeling safe.

Fifty-Seven

Eliminate Barriers to Getting the Work Done

> Be a yardstick of quality. Some people aren't used to an environment where excellence is expected.
>
> —STEVE JOBS

When addressing productivity issues in the workplace, it's vital to look not just at the performance of your individual team members but beyond them to the barriers that may inadvertently be holding them back from success.

It's just too easy for a leader to get stuck in the mire of blaming personnel for the failure of the group and to ignore basic repairable issues that may be contributing to the breakdown within the team.

Start by looking at your organization as a whole. Have you been clear about the expectations for each person, and do they all know how to perform their roles adequately? Do they have the resources they need to perform their tasks successfully? Would your team members say that their actual job matches what they learned about their position during the recruitment process? Does your culture promote a successful work environment for all? Are you offering enough incentives for employees to feel valued in their roles? Are you giving relevant and timely feedback to help grow your team members? Do they have the opportunity to advance within your company in a suitable time period?

This is just a starting point to uncover what might be holding your team back. As a strong leader, it is your most important task to remove barriers that may be inhibiting your team from being as successful and fulfilled as they can be. If you're unsure what your team members need, ask them.

Fifty-Eight

See the Big Picture

Details create the big picture.

—SANFORD I. WEILL

Leading is about the details, and we've all heard the saying that God is in the details. As a leader, however, you also need to be able to pull back periodically to see the big picture.

I know you're already good at seeing the big picture. Bear with me. Seeing the big picture means being able to remove yourself from what you're working on long enough to suspend judgment and see clearly where you're heading. Not where you hope you're heading but where you are truly heading.

It's like having a mate whom your friends don't like but you're absolutely convinced is amazing and not being able to see what they're seeing. If you suspend your own opinion for a minute and look with open curiosity, what are the factors that might be contributing to their perspective?

When you put this into leadership terms, it's about removing yourself enough to strip away your hopes, desires, and dreams for the team and really look at what's there—the good, the bad, and the ugly of it all.

It might help to talk it through with an objective party, like a coach or a friend who is grounded enough not to collude with your perspective.

Fifty-Nine

Be Courageous

Courage is what it takes to stand up and speak;
courage is also what it takes to sit down and
listen.

—WINSTON CHURCHILL

C ourage is often defined as the willingness to confront one's own fears in order to accomplish a greater purpose. Courage (or fortitude) is also considered to be one of the four cardinal virtues in ancient Greek philosophy. In leadership, this is a familiar state of being.

Being courageous in the face of your inner fears is something you'll need to do, sometimes on a daily basis. You'll need to consciously identify whether your inner fear is holding you back or warning you of real danger.

To do that, you'll need to take inner stock of your feelings, gauge when each is at play, and determine how to tell the difference. Once you've done this, learn to trust that you know the difference between an irrational fear, which we all have from time to time, and a real danger. Then you can confidently identify when to take the courageous step into the unknown and move toward your purpose.

One last thing about courage: courage is not synonymous with fear-lessness. It is the ability to be brave in the face of fear.

Sixty

Hire the Right People for the Job

The main way to reduce stress in the workplace is by picking the right people.

—Jesse Schell

Eight out of ten of my coaching sessions with leaders revolve around challenges they have with people who are unable to perform their duties at an expected level. Unfortunately, there is often a snowball effect on the rest of the team, as others may feel resentful or angry with the person who isn't performing well.

As a strong leader, it's vital that you put a lot of energy into the recruitment process because it is an extremely important factor in the success or failure of your team. Put your ego aside, and choose the right person for the right job rather than the person whom you or your board members like.

Ask yourself: Does this person have the skills and attributes it takes for this particular position? How will he or she fit into the team culture? Does he or she understand what it takes physically and mentally to perform this job, and does he or she have the right attitude and desire to be here? Does he or she have the right motivation, compensation, and resources to be successful at his or her duties, and does he or she clearly know what is expected of him or her in this position?

Hiring the right person to come into your workplace family is like bringing someone into your household. Take the time to choose wisely, and look with open eyes at who is right in front of you, not whom you want them to be.

Sixty-One

Be Aware of Your Strengths

> In the midst of winter, I found there was, within me, an invincible summer.
>
> —ALBERT CAMUS

It's important to know your strengths so that you can build on them. I'm sure you've become aware of most of your strengths as you've made your way in the world as a leader, but which areas of strength might you not be seeing?

This is a good time to ask for honest feedback so that you can learn about how others see you. You might be surprised to find that you have strengths that you previously weren't aware of.

For example, one of my clients was criticized by her peers for consistently asking a myriad of questions in meetings. Her leader told her that she often holds back the team because of the time it takes to go through her questions. During her 360-degree feedback, her boss was sure she would hear the same criticism from others in her department. What they found was that her teammates saw her willingness to raise the difficult questions they themselves didn't feel comfortable asking as bravery. Both my client and her boss were made aware that, in their environment, my client was able to be a voice for the team. This new knowledge led the boss to make some changes in her own behaviour so that others in the team could feel safe voicing their concerns.

The bottom line is that you may not see your strengths as clearly as others do. Asking for feedback is a great way to help you learn about your known and hidden strengths.

Sixty-Two

Be Respected

You can demand courtesy but you have to earn respect.

—LAWRENCE GOLDSTONE

How can you tell good leaders in five minutes or less? Walk around their environment, and watch how people relate to them. Do people relate to them easily? Are they personable with the people they lead? Are they approachable? Do they seem to care for the people around them? In short, are they respected?

Being respected is a "tell" for good leadership because it shows that you have earned the trust of the people around you; therefore, they will be open to following your direction. You've done the hard work and earned their trust and respect, and now they allow you to lead and influence them. I say the word "allow" because it's true; if you haven't earned your team members' trust, then they will (consciously or not) throw roadblocks your way.

You may believe that leadership can happen even through fear and intimidation, but how long do you think that would work? In this type of leadership, the people around you will work tirelessly to resist your leadership and campaign to revolutionary heights to make your path impossible until such a time that you fail.

In short, you can't lead without people. Be good to them if you want to succeed.

Sixty-Three

Encourage New Ways of Being

As we look ahead into the next century, leaders will be those who empower others.

—BILL GATES

Strong leaders build on current and past successes while being aware of new trends and new ways of being in their field. Bill Gates is one such leader. Creator of the software industry, he always looked beyond the now and into the next way of being in order to innovate. His drive to create new technology and his success in bringing the right people together to develop history-changing inventions in the computer field are an inspiration for leaders.

Today, Bill Gates still innovates through his philanthropic work for global health care and the reduction of poverty. He encourages politicians and citizens alike to believe that we can live in a world where poverty is a thing of the past and where health care for all is a thing of the future.

To be the kind of leader who encourages new ways of being, surround yourself with people who are visionaries. Encourage them to help your team learn about new innovations and new ways of being so that your team can be on the leading edge of change.

Sixty-Four

See Past the Words
to the Meaning

Don't listen to what I say. Listen to what I mean.

—UNKNOWN

This has to do with your level of EQ. Yes, you've got leadership skills, and you have an amazing education to back it up; but how strong are you emotionally when it comes to dealing with people?

When you're in the business of leading people, you need to steer clear of jumping to conclusions or making up stories about others. It's vital that you hone the ability to listen past the words people are saying to the meaning.

For example, one executive I worked with kept getting stuck in the fact that her team complained constantly about a fellow employee who would watch movies on her iPad during her breaks. They thought this employee was rude and not engaging with others on the team, and they even went so far as to say she was "dumbing herself down" with these awful movies.

After coaching the executive to move beyond her preconceptions, she was able to see that her team members were stating their value of community and strong ties to each other. They wanted to connect with their fellow teammate but felt rejected, so they rejected her as well. The executive went on to have a conversation with the movie-watching employee, who was shocked at the impact she was having on the team. She had not intended to remove herself from the team; instead, she had been using the time to honour her need for downtime as an introvert and recharge from her stressful job.

Listen past the words, and look for the meaning instead of falling into judgments.

Sixty-Five

Be Aware of Others' Skills and Talents

> Before you are a leader, success is all about growing yourself. When you become a leader, success is all about growing others.

—Jack Welch

A big part of leadership is developing other leaders among your team. It's important, therefore, that you keep up to speed about your team members' skills and talents. Take time to notice what's going on around you, and look for positive behaviour in all members of your group, not just in the ones you like personally.

Notice where growth is taking place, and acknowledge it so that individual makes a concerted effort to continue growing in that direction. Let individuals know that you are aware of them and are interested in building their capacities.

Where you notice a decline or stagnation in behaviour, check in with that team member to find out what might be causing it. It could be as simple as not having the right resources to do the job, or it could be that something is happening in his or her personal life that you aren't aware of.

Whatever the reason, it's important to check in periodically with individuals and help them stay aligned with the team.

Notice, acknowledge, and grow your people in an authentic, caring way.

Sixty-Six

Practice Forgiveness

The weak can never forgive. Forgiveness is the attribute of the strong.

—MAHATMA GANDHI

Much too often, we are witness to, or are a part of, some conflict in the workplace. We go through the anxiety of dealing with a negative encounter, bringing others into our story, or even having to address a disciplinary action. We look for others to believe our side of the story, and we desire some type of justice that will give us a sense of completion. What we don't stop to think about is that the other person wants the same thing, too.

Being a strong leader means addressing the conflicts that come up but also teaching your team members the necessary leadership trait of forgiveness. Despite what we've been taught, forgiveness is not a gift that releases the other person in the conflict; it is the gift that releases us. When we are able to let go of the fight or the need to be right, we let go of stress, drama, anxiety, and dis-ease in our body. Hanging on to conflict only brings us personal pain and takes up a lot of energy that could be used for more important things in our lives.

Teaching the value of forgiveness is most probably the best gift you can give to your team members as they move into their own leadership.

It isn't something we talk about much in the organizational world, but it's something that needs to be imparted if we want to create the strong leaders of the future.

Sixty-Seven

Shape Events into Learning Opportunities

Your most unhappy customers are your greatest source of learning.

—BILL GATES

Sometimes your team will suffer loses, and that's a normal part of the way life works. It's crucial that you, as their leader, manage the process all the way through so that the members can move from mourning the loss to seeing a bright future again.

How do you do that? First, allow time and space for mourning. Different people will have different ways of doing this. Let your team members say what they need to say and feel what they need to feel.

After a period of time (not too long), it's time to assess the damage together as a team. What could have prevented it? What is the impact of the loss to your team, your stakeholders, and your future? Where do you go from here?

Without focusing on blame, it's important to do a forensic audit of the event to see what could have been done differently. The aim of this audit is to learn the important lessons that you and your team can use to improve the way you do things and become stronger as a team.

Sixty-Eight

Share Leadership

> You can do what I cannot do. I can do what you
> cannot do. Together we can do great things.

—MOTHER TERESA

Sometimes, you need to be the leader who directs. That's important. You need to know you are good at that, so keep working on being open, clear, and able to have difficult conversations and hold the vision for the team.

Sometimes, however, it's in your best interest to share the leadership. I don't mean give up your leadership. I mean *share* it. In their text *Shared Leadership: Toward a Multi-Level Theory of Leadership*, Craig L. Pearce and Henry P. Sims Jr. describe shared leadership as "leadership that emanates from members of teams and not simply from the appointed leader." This means allowing others to suggest new ways of doing things and letting them take the lead on their suggestions if it benefits the whole team.

You may be thinking that this is hard to do because coaching others to get things done at a high level of professionalism takes too much time, and you just don't have the time to commit to it. The truth is you can't afford not to. If you want to retain good people, you need to trust them to lead, even on a small scale.

People want to grow, and they want to be inspired. Allowing room for them to do this within your team creates confidence, loyalty, trust, and positive morale. Whether it's leading a meeting, an outing, or even an informal conversation, allowing others to lead creates team members who feel valued, and when they feel valued, they are happy to do their best for the team.

Sixty-Nine

Practice Gratefulness

> If you don't like something, change it. If you can't change it, change your attitude.
>
> —MAYA ANGELOU

Your parents may have taught you to say "thank you" to others. They may even have taught you to say "thank you" for all the things you're grateful for, through your daily prayers or meditation. But do you know why being grateful is so fundamentally important to leadership? Gratefulness gives you, as a leader, time to reflect on your journey and reminds you just how far you've come. It helps you notice the positive aspects of your life, and it lessens the laser focus you may tend to point on the mistakes you've made along the way.

Being grateful is a practice in the truest sense of the word, so you need to practice it every day by looking at what's working in your life. Each day, take a moment to find the things that you are grateful for. They can be what you're grateful for that day, month, or year, or they can be what you are grateful for in a situation.

If you find it difficult to come up with something positive, stay with it; reach for it until you find it. Doing this makes you realize that, in every situation, you can see something useful, and from that place, you can build. Your team members need to know you can do this. Sometimes they won't be able to see the positive aspects of a situation, and it will be your job to remind them of it.

As you practice gratefulness, you'll begin to notice that the very language you use will change as your focus changes to what's working in your life. Inadvertently, you may also influence others around you to be grateful as well.

Seventy

Take Ultimate Responsibility for the Team

Whatever happens, take responsibility.

—TONY ROBBINS

The old adage that "the captain goes down with the ship" is a profound way to show how deeply people believe that leaders have to take ultimate responsibility for what happens under their leadership.

Whether in politics or large organizations, it's clear that we are still a people who need to raise leaders up as well as to bring them down when there is a crisis. Many leaders who have seemingly been brought low by a disaster have been able to reinvent themselves and move back into leadership in another sphere. How they are able to survive is not a matter of fate but of their ability to show integrity throughout the crisis and continue to garner trust from stakeholders in a tough situation.

Our organizational society values a leader who is strong enough to take responsibility for his or her actions and his or her team's actions and is able to show humility, grace, and remorse in an authentic way.

Though the captain may indeed go down with the ship in one organization, if the captain is a strong leader, then he or she will undoubtedly be able to captain a team again.

Seventy-One

Be Congruent in Word and Action

> Words may show a man's wit, but actions his meaning.

—BENJAMIN FRANKLIN

When we're talking about being congruent in word and action, what we're really talking about is your reliability as a leader. There used to be a saying in days of old that "your word is your bond," and that's what we expect from our leaders today.

If you say something, your team and your stakeholders need to trust that you'll do your best to make it happen. As I mentioned earlier, you can't influence people unless they trust you, and they will trust you when you act in a trustworthy manner. So do your best to be congruent in your word and actions.

But what happens when you give your word as your bond and things change? You speak to your team and stakeholders honestly and up front as soon as you know that there is a change and that you have a plan to address that change. Let people know what has changed and why the goal has to be altered. If you've already created an atmosphere of trust based on your good record, then most people will choose to believe that you truly are doing your best to live by your word. If there is mistrust about the new phase, then show them by your deeds.

Seventy-Two

Don't Strive for Perfection

The universe doesn't allow perfection.

—STEPHEN HAWKING

Doesn't every leader need to strive for perfection? No. Every leader should strive to do his or her best. Strong leaders understand that this differs greatly from needing to be perfect.

When we think of perfection, we think about finishing the tasks we set out to accomplish in exactly the way we meant to accomplish them. That rarely happens in reality. Sometimes we are lucky enough to reach our goals, but often we get there through a process of successes and failures, not just successes.

Our plan for a perfect course of action is difficult to attain, but if we are open to learning, then we can reach our goals by adapting in the moment and making changes that lead us to our goal.

Strong leaders keep on learning and aren't afraid of making mistakes in order to adapt. Keep reaching for better ways of being and better ways of doing things, but be careful about holding yourself to an ideal that is more destructive than helpful.

Allow room for mistakes. Some of the best inventions, such as penicillin, the pacemaker, and the slinky, have come from them. Be easy on yourself with your expectations. Let go of the burden of reaching for something that doesn't exist. You are enough. Strive only to be your best self.

Seventy-Three

Know When to Walk Away

I didn't give up; I walked away. I had enough of accepting actions that were less than I deserved.

—Nikki Rowe

Here's an unpopular thought but one that all leaders need to consider: Do you know when it's in the best interest of your team for you to leave? How aware are you of your impact on the team or stakeholders who follow you?

I know this isn't something you want to hear, but I'm going to say it because it's important: strong leaders need to assess whether or not they may have overstayed their leadership.

In the case of the formidable Nelson Mandela, he relinquished his power after serving only one term as South Africa's president, even though he was popular enough to have continued in that role indefinitely.

As leaders, we want to see things through until their completion, and, a lot of times, that means staying with a project or team until we reach the end goal that we hold in our personal vision. Our personal vision of completion may not be in service to the group, however.

Goals need to be driven by the team and the leader—not just by the leader. Strong leaders understand that, though they play an important role, what might be needed is for one leader to create the vision, another to move it forward, and yet another to reach the goal. It's important to recognize where you fit and when it's time to leave.

Seventy-Four

Understand that Leadership Is a Journey

The more I live, the more I learn. The more I learn, the more I realize the less I know.

—Michel Legrand

Leadership is not a destination; it's a lifelong journey. Becoming a leader means that you are being trusted to take care of others, whether there are two or twenty thousand people in your team. It means that others trust you to have their best interest in mind and will follow you as long as you are worthy of their partnership.

Sometimes you will do great things and make great decisions. Sometimes you will make troubling decisions and have a less-than-positive impact on the team and the organizational climate. What makes you a strong leader is that you recognize when you are doing well and take the time to honour that—and you recognize when you have made a mistake and are willing to own up to it.

You are also willing to be vulnerable enough to make those mistakes, which means that you are modelling how to be an emotionally intelligent leader for your team members. You are also a strong leader because you take your job seriously and remind yourself often that you are being charged with inspiring others, engaging others, and influencing others to make good decisions for their future and the future of the company. You are willing to do the dirty work if needed and model the new changes that come. You are a great leader because you are willing to learn and do better when you know better.

Leadership is a lifelong journey, and you are a strong leader because you know this and you forgive yourself, pace yourself, and celebrate the path.

Seventy-Five

Adapt

Intelligence is the ability to adapt to change.

—STEPHEN HAWKING

In my work with leaders, I often get asked, What is the one trait that all strong leaders should possess? After all these years in the field, I find that question easy to answer because I come across it time and again without fail.

All strong leaders should be able to adapt.

No matter who or what you're leading, you need to be able to adapt with changes that come your way in order for you to remain relevant to the team and to the vision of success your team has laid out. Some changes that come may not be welcome, but they come nonetheless. Some changes are exciting and bring a lot of great energy. Either way, you as a leader have to be able to adapt to these changes in order to bridge the gap between what was and what will be. Your team will look to you for answers as to how they should manage new changes, and it's incumbent on you to be five steps ahead of your team and to look to the future beyond the change.

Adapting means being able to innovate with new input by accessing the wisdom of the past and the vision of the future. Lean on others in your team: your pioneers who hold the vision, your wise ones who hold the cultural expectations (of the past), and your individuals who see the present as successful. Work with all of them to design the map of your future and the steps you'll take to adapt to that path.

My Leadership Action Plan

Use, change, and add to it as needed.

What five leadership traits do I already possess?

1.
2.
3.
4.
5.

What two leadership traits do I want to add to my leadership capacity this year?

1.
2.

What is one thing that I am willing to do this week/month to develop each of my new leadership traits?

   This could be informal learning, reading a related article, reading a specific book, finding a useful resource, watching a TED Talks video, taking a formal course, going to a conference, getting a coach, writing a book, and so on.

1.

2.

How will I know that I am successful in my new leadership abilities?

This can include sharing your goal with others and asking if they are noticing a change, asking coworkers for direct feedback, keeping a journal and noticing when you've utilized the trait in specific situations, and so on.

1.

2.

3.

How will I commemorate my hard work and development in my new leadership competencies?

This might include sharing your story with others in a meeting, writing an article for publication on your leadership journey, being a guest blogger, adding new skills to your resume, and so on.

About the Author

Since 1998 TC Waisman has been coaching executive leaders on how to achieve personal greatness…or at least to enjoy a hell-of-a-worthy life. She hails from a dot on the map (Fiji) and was inspired to write her Masters thesis on the ancient wisdom of the South Pacific that can be applied in a transformational way to the organizational world.

Failing dismally at all things domestic, TC's path in academics and leadership turned out to be a good fit. Miraculously organizations are finding her quirky brand of humour, unruly afro and charming sarcasm excellent public speaking tools.

TC resides in Vancouver, Canada and credits her fierce, resilient clients with helping her uncover the traits that make up great leaders.